Collins

Key Stage 3
Islam

Robert Orme
Series Editor: Robert Orme

Published by Collins
An imprint of HarperCollins*Publishers*
The News Building
1 London Bridge Street
London SE1 9GF

10 9 8 7 6 5 4

ISBN 978-0-00-822772-2

A catalogue record for this book is available from the British Library

Publisher: Joanna Ramsay
Editor: Hannah Dove
Author: Robert Orme
Series Editor: Robert Orme
Development Editor: Sonya Newland
Project manager: Emily Hooton
Copy-editor: Jill Morris
Image researcher: Shelley Noronha
Proof-reader: Nikky Twyman
Cover designer: We Are Laura
Cover image: Zoran Karapancev/Shutterstock
Production controller: Rachel Weaver
Typesetter: QBS
Printed and bound by CPI Group (UK) Ltd, Croydon, CR0 4YY

Contents

Introduction

It is not easy to define what makes something a religion. In some religions one god is worshipped, in others many gods are worshipped, and in some no god is worshipped at all. Some religions have a single founder. In others, there is not one person who starts it or one clear moment when it began. To make things more complicated, there are often strong differences of opinion between and even within particular religions. Two people following the same religion can believe opposing things and follow their religion in strikingly different ways. Within any religion, some people build their whole lives around their beliefs while others are less committed to their religion but still think of themselves as part of it. Followers of all religions believe that they have found truth, but their ideas about what is true differ greatly.

Approximately 84 per cent of people in the world today follow a religion and experts predict that this will rise to 87 per cent by 2050. The most followed religion in the UK is Christianity, but there are also followers of many other religions including Islam, Judaism, Buddhism, Hinduism and Sikhism. In recent times there has also been a big increase in the number of people in the UK who do not follow any religion. Some are atheists which means that they do not believe there is a god or gods. Others are agnostics meaning they are not sure if a god or gods exists. Others might believe there is a god or gods, but choose not to belong to a religion.

By studying the beliefs and ways of life of millions of people around the world, you will gain a greater understanding of the past, the modern world and humanity itself. You will explore questions that have troubled humankind through the ages and examine the diverse ways in which these questions have been answered. In a world where religion has and continues to play such a large role, the importance of understanding it is as great as ever.

Robert Orme (Series Editor)

Concise topic introductions set the scene and focus your learning.

Engaging photos illustrate the key ideas.

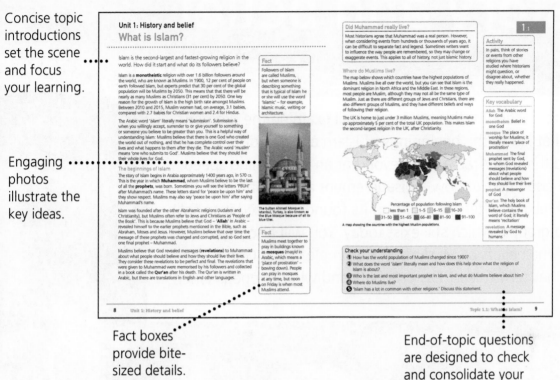

Fact boxes provide bite-sized details.

End-of-topic questions are designed to check and consolidate your understanding.

Key fact boxes help you to revise and remember the main points from each unit.

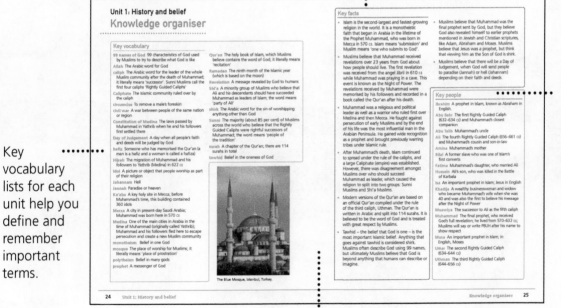

Key people boxes summarise the key figures in the religion

Key vocabulary lists for each unit help you define and remember important terms.

Knowledge organisers can be used to revise and quiz yourself on key dates, definitions and descriptions.

History and belief

In this first section of this book, you will examine the dramatic events that led to the beginnings of Islam and will discover how it spread through Arabia and beyond at an astonishing speed. You will also find out how a disagreement about who should lead the religion after the death of its founder caused it to split into two groups, which still exist today. You will also explore some of the beliefs of Muslims, for example, what God is like, who he has sent to earth as prophets and what happens when we die.

Unit 1: History and belief

What is Islam?

Islam is the second-largest and fastest-growing religion in the world. How did it start and what do its followers believe?

Islam is a **monotheistic** religion with over 1.6 billion followers around the world, who are known as Muslims. In 1900, 12 per cent of people on earth followed Islam, but experts predict that 30 per cent of the global population will be Muslims by 2050. This means that that there will be nearly as many Muslims as Christians (31 per cent) by 2050. One key reason for the growth of Islam is the high birth rate amongst Muslims. Between 2010 and 2015, Muslim women had, on average, 3.1 babies, compared with 2.7 babies for Christian women and 2.4 for Hindus.

The Arabic word '*islam*' literally means 'submission'. Submission is when you willingly accept, surrender to or give yourself to something or someone you believe to be greater than you. This is a helpful way of understanding Islam: Muslims believe that there is one God who created the world out of nothing, and that he has complete control over their lives and what happens to them after they die. The Arabic word '*muslim*' means 'one who submits to God'. Muslims believe that they should live their whole lives for God.

The beginnings of Islam

The story of Islam begins in Arabia approximately 1400 years ago, in 570 CE. This is the year in which **Muhammad**, whom Muslims believe to be the last of all the **prophets**, was born. Sometimes you will see the letters 'PBUH' after Muhammad's name. These letters stand for 'peace be upon him' and they show respect. Muslims may also say 'peace be upon him' after saying Muhammad's name.

Islam was founded after the other Abrahamic religions (Judaism and Christianity), but Muslims often refer to Jews and Christians as 'People of the Book'. This is because Muslims believe that God – '**Allah**' in Arabic – revealed himself to the earlier prophets mentioned in the Bible, such as Abraham, Moses and Jesus. However, Muslims believe that over time the message of these prophets was changed and corrupted, and so God sent one final prophet – Muhammad.

Muslims believe that God revealed messages (**revelations**) to Muhammad about what people should believe and how they should live their lives. They consider these revelations to be perfect and final. The revelations that were given to Muhammad were memorised by his followers and collected in a book called the **Qur'an** after his death. The Qur'an is written in Arabic, but there are translations in English and other languages.

The Sultan Ahmed Mosque in Istanbul, Turkey, is also known as the Blue Mosque because of all its blue tiles.

Did Muhammad really live?

Most historians agree that Muhammad was a real person. However, when considering events from hundreds or thousands of years ago, it can be difficult to separate fact and legend. Sometimes writers want to influence the way people are remembered, so they may change or exaggerate events. This applies to all of history, not just Islamic history.

Where do Muslims live?

The map below shows which countries have the highest populations of Muslims. Muslims live all over the world, but you can see that Islam is the dominant religion in North Africa and the Middle East. In these regions, most people are Muslim, although they may not all be the same type of Muslim. Just as there are different groups of Jews and Christians, there are also different groups of Muslims, and they have different beliefs and ways of following their religion.

The UK is home to just under 3 million Muslims, meaning Muslims make up approximately 5 per cent of the total UK population. This makes Islam the second-largest religion in the UK, after Christianity.

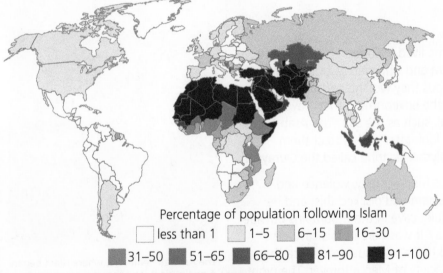

Percentage of population following Islam

less than 1 | 1–5 | 6–15 | 16–30
31–50 | 51–65 | 66–80 | 81–90 | 91–100

A map showing the countries with the highest Muslim populations.

Key vocabulary

Allah The Arabic word for God

monotheism Belief in one God

mosque The place of worship for Muslims; it literally means 'place of prostration'

Muhammad The final prophet sent by God, to whom God revealed messages (revelations) about what people should believe and how they should live their lives

prophet A messenger of God

Qur'an The holy book of Islam, which Muslims believe contains the word of God; it literally means 'recitation'

revelation A message revealed by God to humans

Check your understanding

1. How has the world population of Muslims changed since 1900?
2. What does the word 'islam' literally mean and how does this help show what the religion of Islam is about?
3. Who is the last and most important prophet in Islam, and what do Muslims believe about him?
4. Where do Muslims live?
5. 'Islam has a lot in common with other religions.' Discuss this statement.

Unit 1: History and belief
How did Islam begin?

How did Muhammad's encounter with the angel Jibril in a cave near Mecca begin a new religion and alter the course of history?

The early life of Muhammad

At the time of Muhammad, there were two main cities in central Arabia – **Medina** and **Mecca** (sometimes spelled 'Madinah' and 'Makkah'). Muhammad was born in Mecca in 570 CE. His father, Abdullah, died before he was born and his mother, Amina, died when he was six, so Muhammad was brought up by his uncle, Abu Talib, who was a trader. Muhammad would accompany his uncle on business trips across the Arabian desert to Syria and gained a reputation as an excellent trader. He was given the nickname al-Amin, which means 'the trustworthy'. At the age of 25, Muhammad married a wealthy businesswoman and widow called Khadija. She was 15 years older than him, but she admired the skills he had learned from his uncle.

Arabia before Islam

Most people in Arabia at this time lived in tribes. Some of these people were followers of Judaism and Christianity, but many tribes were **polytheistic**. The gods they worshipped were often linked to nature and aspects of the environment that played an essential part in people's survival, such as the sun. The Arab tribes believed that these gods would look after and protect them. Muhammad was born into a polytheistic tribe called the Quraysh.

In the seventh century, there was much cruelty, violence and poverty in the city of Mecca. Muhammad disliked this, and he would often retreat to a cool, quiet cave in the mountains outside the city in order to think and pray. It was here in this cave, at the age of 40, that Muhammad had a religious experience that would change his life and the society of Mecca forever. The night on which this happened is called Laylat al-Qadr in Arabic, which can be translated as the Night of Power.

The Arabian Peninsula, where Islam began. A peninsula is land that is surrounded by water on three sides.

The Night of Power

On this night, the angel Jibril (Gabriel) appeared to Muhammad and revealed a message from God. Jibril told Muhammad to recite words that were later recorded in the Qur'an.

Islamic scholars disagree about what exactly happened in the cave. According to one account, Jibril told Muhammad to read from a scroll. When Muhammad said that he could not read, Jibril told him three times *'iqra!'* ('Read!'). On the third time, he placed his hands around Muhammad's waist and squeezed him until the words forced their way

> ### Fact
> The Night of Power is celebrated by Muslims towards the end of the month of **Ramadan**. Muslims will often stay awake praying, as they believe that God is especially forgiving on this night.

into Muhammad's mouth. It was as though the words were being written on his heart and he would never forget them.

Muhammad was still shaking when he returned home to Khadija. She knew her husband was an honest man, so his words must truly be from God. She became the first believer of his message. The second person to become a Muslim was Muhammad's cousin, Ali, followed by one of Muhammad's closest friends, Abu Bakr.

A crowd of people visiting the cave where Muhammad is believed to have received his first revelation from Jibril.

The Qur'an

The Arabic word 'qur'an' means 'recitation' or 'that which is read or recited', because this is how Muhammad received the words. The Night of Power is recorded in **surah** 96 of the Qur'an, which is often known as the 'Blood Clot' chapter, because it says that God created humans from a blood clot. Over the next 23 years, Jibril visited Muhammad with more revelations that were remembered and recorded during his lifetime and collected together after his death, according to Islamic sources.

The Night Journey

According to Islamic tradition, one night in approximately 620 CE Muhammad was in Mecca praying when Jibril suddenly appeared and flew him to Jerusalem on a winged horse. Muhammad prayed and spoke with all the prophets that have ever lived. He then ascended to the heavens and spent time with God, who told him that Muslims should pray five times a day. Muhammad then returned to Jerusalem and flew back to Mecca. Muslims disagree about whether the Night Journey really happened or whether Muhammad saw the events in a vision.

Key vocabulary

Mecca A city in present-day Saudi Arabia; Muhammad was born here in 570 CE

Medina One of the main cities in Arabia in the time of Muhammad (originally called Yathrib)

polytheism Belief in many gods

Ramadan The ninth month of the Islamic year (which is based on the moon)

surah A chapter of the Qur'an; there are 114 surahs in total

Check your understanding

1 When was Muhammad born and when was the Night of Power?

2 Describe Muhammad's early life.

3 What was Arabia like before Islam was established there?

4 In your own words, describe what happened on the Night of Power.

5 What was the Night Journey? Explain different views a Muslim might have about this event.

How did Islam rise to influence?

How did Muhammad combine his radical religious message with political and military power?

Muhammad the prophet

After the Night of Power, Muhammad began preaching his message in Mecca. His words were considered radical. Muhammad said that it was wrong for Meccans to worship many gods. He insisted that there was only one God, and claimed that this God had given him instructions for how people should live their lives. In particular, he criticised the worship of **idols**.

This was particularly controversial because Muhammad's own tribe looked after the idols in Mecca's main holy site, the **Ka'aba**. The leaders of the tribe did not like Muhammad's radical monotheistic message. They saw it as a threat to their power and to the income they earned through polytheistic tribes visiting the Ka'aba on pilgrimage. They tried to persuade him to abandon his preaching and to join them as the most powerful traders in Mecca. When Muhammad refused, the leaders of the tribe denied Muhammad's message and persecuted his followers. They banned Meccans from marrying or trading with any of Muhammad's followers. Some of them were tortured and killed.

A modern picture of the Ka'aba.

Bilal

One man who was attacked because of his conversion to Islam was a slave called Bilal. He was one of Muhammad's earliest followers. When Bilal's master found out that he had converted to Islam he violently tortured him, but Bilal would not give up his faith. His master was angry that Bilal regarded God as more important than him and that Bilal would not honour the many idols that the other Meccans worshipped. His master ordered that a large stone be placed on Bilal's chest to slowly crush him. Bilal simply said, 'Ahad, ahad' – 'God is one.' Muhammad was shocked when he heard about the treatment of Bilal and told his friend Abu Bakr to buy Bilal from his master. After Bilal was freed from slavery, he became a close friend of Muhammad.

Bilal became an important figure in early Islam. Here, he is calling Muslims to pray from the top of the Ka'aba.

Muhammad the politician

In 620 CE, while preaching outside Mecca, Muhammad met six men from the city of Yathrib (Medina). They had heard the message of Islam and became Muslims. Polytheist, Jewish and Christian tribes all lived in Yathrib, and they had all been fighting each other for many years. The six men asked Muhammad to move to Yathrib to help settle the conflicts. Over the next two years, more people from Yathrib visited Muhammad, pledging allegiance to him and inviting him to move to their city. In 622 CE, after years

Fact

Yathrib was later named al-Madinat al-Nabi, 'the city of the Prophet'. Today it is known as Medina.

of persecution in Mecca, Muhammad instructed all his followers to travel 320 kilometres (200 miles) north to Yathrib. The emigration of Muhammad and his followers to Medina, as Yathrib became known, is called the **Hijrah**.

One of the first things that Muhammad did when he arrived in Medina was to write the **Constitution of Medina**. This was a set of religious laws that aimed to bring together the Muslim, Jewish, Christian and polytheist tribes who lived there and create a fairer society. It included rules to help widows and orphans and it said that Medina should be a 'sacred place' where no weapons could be carried. This was Muhammad's first attempt at creating a community based on his religious beliefs, and Medina became the first Islamic city-state.

Muhammad the warrior

At the time of Muhammad, there were many violent disputes between tribes across the Arabian Peninsula. In 624 CE, Muslims in Medina were being persecuted by tribes in Mecca. Muhammad led his army of followers into battle to defend the safety of Muslims in Medina against this violence. The Battle of Badr, as this event became known, confirmed that Muhammad was no longer just a prophet and a politician – he was also a strong warrior. As a result of his victory in this battle, more people in Medina accepted Muhammad's authority.

After a series of battles between Mecca and Medina, Muhammad finally conquered Mecca in 629 CE. Muhammad had sent a message in advance saying that those who stayed in their homes when his army entered the city would not be harmed. On entering Mecca, Muhammad rode straight for the Ka'aba. He circled it seven times before entering it and destroying all the idols inside of it. He then dedicated the Ka'aba to God.

By the end of Muhammad's life, he was the most influential man in Arabia. He had successfully united the warring tribes of the region under Islamic rule. All of the polytheistic tribes had become Muslims, as well as some of the Jews. Muhammad had combined his radical religious message with political and military power. The world would never be the same again.

The Battle of Badr occurred in Medina.

Key vocabulary

Constitution of Medina The laws passed by Muhammad in Yathrib when he and his followers first settled there

Hijrah The emigration of Muhammad and his followers to Yathrib (Medina) in 622 CE

idol A picture or object that people worship as part of their religion

Ka'aba A holy site in Mecca which Muhammad dedicated to God after destroying its 360 idols

Activity

Make a timeline showing the key dates in the life of Muhammad. Include his birth, marriage, the Night of Power, the Hijrah, the Battle of Badr, conquering Mecca, and Muhammad's death in 632 CE.

Check your understanding

1. Why did Muhammad disapprove of idol worship?
2. How did the leaders of Muhammad's tribe react when he told them there was one true God?
3. Describe what happened to Bilal.
4. What was the Constitution of Medina?
5. Was Muhammad a prophet, a politician or a warrior? Explain your answer fully.

Unit 1: History and belief
Why did Islam split?

How did a disagreement about Muhammad's rightful successor cause Islam to split?

The caliphs

Muhammad died in June 632 CE. His message had spread at a rapid pace, and by the time of his death he had conquered the entire Arabian Peninsula and was widely regarded as a true prophet. In the 30 years after Muhammad's death, the Muslim community was led by four political and religious rulers (**caliphs**), all of whom had been close companions of Muhammad:

1. Abu Bakr (632–634 CE)
2. Umar (634–644 CE)
3. Uthman (644–656 CE)
4. Ali (656–661 CE)

Under these four caliphs, the religion of Islam spread across the world at an astonishing speed. This happened through people converting and invasion.

By 750 CE, the Islamic Empire stretched from the westernmost point of Spain to the eastern edge of India. This empire was known as the **Caliphate** and continued to be ruled over by a succession of caliphs in the centuries that followed.

Abu Bakr

After Muhammad's death, some tribes in the Arabian Peninsula wanted to return to having their own rulers. There were also disagreements between followers of Islam, which threatened to divide the new religious community. The first caliph, Abu Bakr, wanted to make sure that people living in Arabia remained Muslims and lived under Islamic rule. During his reign he often used force to defeat rebellions against him and maintain power.

Abu Bakr, the first caliph was a friend of Muhammad and an early convert to Islam.

Umar's conversion

According to Islamic tradition, the second caliph, Umar, originally despised the new religion of Islam and wanted to murder Muhammad. On his way to carry out this attack, Umar stopped at his sister's house to let her and her husband know what he thought about them becoming Muslims. However, when Umar heard them recite the words of the Qur'an, he converted to Islam on the spot and became a loyal follower of Muhammad. As caliph, he helped Islam expand beyond Arabia, conquering the areas now known as Palestine, Syria, Iraq, Egypt and Iran.

Islam continued to spread fast during Uthman's 12-year rule. Uthman had many supporters, but there were also rebels living in the Caliphate who were opposed to him being leader. This caused violence to break out between different groups of Muslims. In 656 CE, opponents of Uthman broke into his house carrying swords and assassinated him.

The fourth caliph, Ali, was Muhammad's cousin – he was the son of Abu Talib. He was also married to Muhammad's daughter Fatima, making him Muhammad's son-in-law. Ali was elected to lead the community after Uthman had been assassinated, but, despite him being a relative of Muhammad, Ali had many opponents who he had to fight to secure power. One of these was a man called Muawiya, the Muslim governor of Syria, who felt that Ali had not done enough to take revenge on Uthman's killers. Muawiya's opposition to Ali led to a war in which different groups of Muslims fought each other for power. In 661 CE, Ali was assassinated, and Muawiya became the fifth caliph.

Pilgrims and scholars at the shrine of Ali.

Sunni and Shi'a Muslims

After Muhammad's death, there was disagreement amongst Muslims over who should be their leader. Not everyone agreed that Abu Bakr, Umar and Uthman should have been caliphs, and this caused Islam to split into two groups and its followers to become known as **Sunni** Muslims and **Shi'a** Muslims.

The majority of Muslims in the world today (about 85 per cent) are Sunni. They believe that it was correct for Abu Bakr to become leader after Muhammad, because he was Muhammad's closest companion. They also think that Umar, Uthman and Ali were the right people to succeed Abu Bakr. However, there is disagreement amongst Sunni Muslims about whether the caliphs who ruled in the centuries after these four men – who are sometimes known as the four Rightly Guided Caliphs – were rightful rulers.

Shi'a Muslims believe that God told Muhammad that Ali should be his immediate successor and that Muhammad made this clear to his followers in a speech given in the year of his death, 632 CE. They believe that the first three caliphs should not have been the rulers of Muslims. Shi'a Muslims also believe that, after Ali's death, his son Hussein should have succeeded him, not Muawiya, and that leadership of Muslims should have continued to pass down through the descendants of Ali.

Key vocabulary

caliph The Arabic word for the leader of the whole Muslim community after the death of Muhammad; it literally means 'successor'. Sunni Muslims call the first four caliphs 'Rightly Guided Caliphs'

Caliphate The Islamic community ruled over by the caliph

Shi'a A smaller group of Muslims who believe that Ali and his descendants should have succeeded Muhammad as leaders of Islam

Sunni The majority (about 85 per cent) of Muslims across the world who believe that the Rightly Guided Caliphs were rightful successors of Muhammad

Check your understanding

1 What did Abu Bakr do while he was caliph?

2 How did Umar initially feel about Islam and what did he achieve as caliph?

3 Why was there a war between Muslims during Ali's rule?

4 Do Sunni and Shi'a Muslims agree on who should have succeeded Muhammad? Explain your answer.

5 "The caliphs played an important role in the development of Islam." Discuss this statement.

Unit 1: History and belief
What is the Qur'an?

What is in the Qur'an and why is it important to Muslims?

The Qur'an is the most important holy book for Muslims. They believe that it was revealed to Muhammad by God. It is seen as the perfect, literal word of God that gives people guidance on how they should live their lives. The Arabic word *'qur'an'* literally means 'recitation' (saying something aloud). According to tradition, Muhammad could not read, but on the Night of Power the angel Jibril insisted, saying, 'Read!' – *'iqra'!* – three times. Muhammad received a rush of energy and suddenly he was able to repeat the words aloud.

Muslims believe that the beauty and power of the Qur'an can only be fully experienced when it is recited aloud, because this is how it was received by Muhammad. As such, when Muslims read the Qur'an, they do so out loud. Huge respect is given to those who can learn the Qur'an by heart. They are given the special title **hafiz** and will sometimes perform the entire Qur'an to other Muslims. Muslims think that the Qur'an can only be truly read in Arabic, because this was the language spoken by Muhammad when he received it. When the Qur'an is translated, it is no longer the words recited by Muhammad. Translations of the Qur'an, therefore, are seen only as interpretations of or substitutes for the Qur'an, not the holy book itself.

This fragment of the Qur'an, owned by the University of Birmingham, is thought to be one of the oldest in the world. The text is written on sheep – or goatskin and may even have been written by someone who knew Muhammad.

How is the Qur'an arranged?

Muhammad received the Qur'an over a 23-year period of his life. Many Islamic scholars are interested in finding out when Muhammad received particular revelations. In Mecca, Muhammad and his followers were being persecuted, whereas in Medina they had the opportunity to establish their own community, and this is reflected in the revelations received.

Initially, the Qur'an was not written down, but was memorised and passed between people by word of mouth. However, towards the end of his life, Muhammad started to dictate chapters (surahs) to his companions so that they could write them down. These chapters would have originally been written down on pieces of animal bone, leather and palm leaves. Each of the 114 surahs is split into verses. In total, there are over 6000 verses in the Qur'an.

Chapters in the Christian Bible move chronologically through time, like a story. In the Qur'an, however, the surahs are generally arranged in order of length, with the longer surahs at the beginning and the shorter ones at the end. This can be a little confusing – for example, the surah that was revealed first to Muhammad is surah 96.

> **Fact**
>
> After Muhammad's death, the third caliph, Uthman, was worried about the Qur'an changing as new followers recited it in newly conquered regions. He created an official Qur'an and ordered that all other versions should be destroyed. All modern versions of the Qur'an are based on this official Qur'an.

Each surah is named after an object or a subject within it. For example, surah 2 is called 'The Cow', because in it Moses tells people to sacrifice a cow. Surah 29 is called 'The Spider' and surah 35 is called 'The Creator'. The most important surah is the first, 'The Opening', which Muslims must recite five times each day. You can read this surah on page 18.

The perfect word

Some parts of the Qur'an are similar to stories found in Jewish and Christian holy books. However, Muslims believe these contain inaccuracies, so God gave Muhammad his perfect word in order to correct them. Muslims believe that Muhammad is the final prophet, whose message has been recorded with complete accuracy in the Qur'an. There will be no further prophets or revelations from God.

Respecting the Qur'an

In order to show respect to the Qur'an, Muslims will often wash before touching it, and will keep it in a clean place with nothing on top of or above it. The Qur'an should be the only book on the top shelf of a bookcase. It is never placed on the floor and if someone drops or damages it, then he or she might kiss it as a sign of respect. Old, worn-out copies should not be thrown away. Most Muslims agree that old Qur'ans should either be wrapped in cloth and buried deep in the ground or placed in flowing water, weighed down with a heavy stone.

The Qu'ran.

Key vocabulary

hafiz Someone who has memorised the Qur'an (a man is a hafiz and a woman is called a hafiza)

Check your understanding

1 What does the Arabic word *'qur'an'* mean?
2 In what language must the Qur'an be recited and why?
3 How was the Qur'an originally passed between people and recorded?
4 Describe two differences between the Qur'an and the Bible.
5 How do Muslims show respect to the Qur'an?

Unit 1: History and belief
What do Muslims believe about God?

Muslims believe that God is beyond human understanding, so how do they try to describe him?

When Islam began, most people in Mecca were polytheists, worshipping gods linked to nature or the environment. When Muhammad began preaching that there was only one God, it made him unpopular with leaders of his tribe, who were responsible for the Ka'aba and looked after its 360 idols. Muhammad said that there should be no idols and destroyed those in the Ka'aba when he conquered Mecca in 629 CE. Therefore, monotheism – the belief that there is only one God – lies at the very heart of Islam.

What is God like?

Muslims believe that there is nothing greater than God. No words can come close to explaining what God is like – he is beyond anything that humans can think or say. However, Muslims believe that God has revealed some of his characteristics in the Qur'an and other sayings of Muhammad. These characteristics are known as the **99 names of God**. Some of these can be seen in surah 1 below.

The Qur'an teaches that God is the eternal creator of everything. He knows everything, he has power over everything, and he decides when people live and die. The first surah of the Qur'an, 'The Opening', shows God's power by describing him as 'Lord' and 'Master':

Many Muslims memorise the 99 names of God so that they can recite them when they pray. This man is using a subhah – a string of prayer beads – to keep count of the 99 names of God.

> 66 In the name of God, the Lord of Mercy, the Giver of Mercy! Praise belongs to God, Lord of all worlds, the Lord of Mercy, the Giver of Mercy, Master of the Day of Judgement. It is you we worship; it is you we ask for help. Guide us to the straight path: the path of those You have blessed, those who incur no anger and who have not gone astray. 99
>
> Qur'an 1:1–7

This first surah also teaches Muslims that God is generous and compassionate. Muslims believe that God is the kindest of all beings, that he loves his creation, and that he will always forgive people for their sins if they are truly sorry. The first surah also teaches that there will be a Day of Judgement, when God will judge all people. Because Muslims believe that God sees everything, they try to live in a way that pleases him.

The first surah of the Qur'an contains seven verses, which emphasise God's greatness and mercy.

Tawhid and shirk

Muslims believe that God is One and there are no Gods other than him. This belief in the oneness of God is called **tawhid**. Anything that goes against tawhid is called **shirk**, which is the Arabic word for the sin of worshipping many gods or idols rather than the one God.

> 66 He is God: there is no god other than Him. It is he who knows what is unseen and what is seen, He is the Lord of Mercy, the Giver of Mercy. He is God: there is no god other than Him, the Controller, the Holy One, Source of Peace, Granter of Security, Guardian over all, the Almighty, the Compeller, the Truly Great; God is far above anything they consider to be His partner. 99
>
> Qur'an 59:22–23

Shirk includes trying to compare something or someone to God or claiming that something is equal to him. For example, if a Muslim said that something was as powerful as God, then this would be shirk. It would also be shirk if a Muslim tried to create a picture or a statue of God. Because God is like nothing on earth, he is beyond human imagination, so making an image of him would be idolatry. The Christian belief in the Trinity would also be seen as shirk, because it states that God exists as Father, Son and Holy Spirit.

Muslims believe that drawing God is shirk. For this reason, it is common for the 99 names of God found in the Qur'an to be written in artistic writing called calligraphy.

Key vocabulary

99 names of God 99 characteristics of God used by Muslims to try to describe what God is like

shirk The Arabic word for the sin of worshipping anything other than God

tawhid Belief in the oneness of God

Check your understanding

1 Why did Muhammad's message about God cause conflict?

2 Explain three things that Muslims believe about God.

3 Explain what Muslims mean by 'tawhid'.

4 Explain what is meant by 'shirk'. Give examples.

5 'It is impossible to describe God.' Discuss this statement.

Who are the prophets in Islam?

The final and most important prophet in Islam is Muhammad, but who were the other prophets?

A prophet is someone who is believed to be a messenger sent by God. Muslims think that the prophets in Judaism and Christianity were sent by God to bring important messages to people on earth. The Qur'an mentions 25 prophets by name, including Abraham, Moses and Jesus. However, Muslims refer to the prophets by their Arabic names, so instead of Abraham, Moses and Jesus you will hear Muslims talk of Ibrahim, Musa and Isa. Muslims believe that this chain of prophets began with Adam in the Garden of Eden. Adam was both the first man and the first prophet. God spoke to him and soon his descendants began to spread over the whole earth.

Muslims believe that the Qur'an is the final and complete revelation from God. It does not contain a completely new message, though – it is a final, corrected, version of the inaccurately recorded teachings of previous prophets. For this reason, the Qur'an often includes additional or different detail when describing events that are also in the Bible.

Abraham (Ibrahim)

Abraham was born in the city of Ur in modern Iraq. At the time, the people of Ur believed in many gods, often linked to the environment. Many of their leaders also claimed that *they* were gods. However, the Qur'an says that Abraham rejected this, believing that there was only one God.

According to Islamic tradition, Abraham met Nimrod, the king of Babylon, who believed that he was a god. However, Nimrod was worried that he was losing power, as more and more of his people were starting to believe in one God. Nimrod wanted to debate with Abraham to show his people that he was a god and that Abraham was a liar. In surah 2 of the Qur'an, it says that Nimrod challenged Abraham's claim that only his God gives life and causes death by saying that he too can do this, perhaps by executing or freeing people. However, when Abraham said that his God makes the sun rise in the east and set in the west, Nimrod had no answer.

Jesus (Isa)

Jesus is viewed with great respect by Muslims and is an important prophet. There is a whole surah in the Qur'an that describes Jesus' miraculous birth to the virtuous virgin Mary. The Qur'an also tells of Jesus's miracles and teachings.

However, there is a significant difference between Muslim and Christian beliefs about Jesus. Muslims do not believe that Jesus died on a cross, but rather that God raised him to heaven alive. Muslims believe that the Qur'an corrects Christian misunderstandings about the nature of Jesus.

> **Fact**
>
> Muslims believe that Adam originally built the Ka'aba and it was later rebuilt by Abraham and his son Ishmael (Ismail). After this, it became misused as a place of pilgrimage for polytheists, who filled it with idols. Muslims believe that Muhammad reclaimed the Ka'aba as a place of worship to the one true God when he conquered Mecca.

Nimrod, the king of Babylon.

For Muslims, he is an important prophet who called people to submit to the one true God, but he is neither divine nor the Son of God, as Christians believe him to be.

Muhammad

Muhammad was born nearly 600 years after Jesus and a long time after Abraham and Moses. Although Muhammad was not divine, he is considered the most special of the prophets. He is often referred to as 'the Seal of all Prophets', or simply as 'the Prophet', to emphasise his importance as the final and most important of God's messengers.

Respecting the prophets

Most Muslims believe that it is disrespectful to show pictures of the prophets, particularly Muhammad. Instead, much Islamic artwork is based on geometric patterns and artistic writing called calligraphy. In a mosque, you will never see pictures of animals, people or God.

In the past, there was Islamic artwork showing the prophets. The first pictures were created by Muslim artists in the thirteenth century and were paid for by the rich and powerful people of the time. The pictures show almost every part of Muhammad's life recorded in the Qur'an. They were made for both Sunni and Shi'a worshippers and examples can be found in major museums and libraries around the world. Despite this, most Muslims in the twenty-first century believe it is wrong to create pictures of prophets.

> **Fact**
>
> In keeping with the tradition started by Abraham, Jews and Muslims **circumcise** boys at a young age. In Judaism, this happens after eight days. Muslim boys are usually circumcised before puberty. Muslims often name their children after prophets like Muhammad and Abraham, or other figures from Islamic history, such as the caliphs.

The inside of the Sheikh Lotfollah Mosque in Iran is decorated with calligraphy and geometric art.

> **Key vocabulary**
>
> **circumcise** To remove a male's foreskin

Check your understanding

1. How many prophets are mentioned in the Qur'an and who was the first?
2. What are the Arabic names given to Abraham, Moses and Jesus?
3. Explain why Nimrod wanted to debate with Abraham and what happened.
4. Explain the differences between Islamic and Christian beliefs about Jesus.
5. 'Prophets should not be drawn.' Discuss this statement.

Unit 1: History and belief
What do Muslims believe happens when we die?

Muslims believe that those who please God will be accepted into paradise, but what will God's judgement be based on?

Heaven and hell

The question of what happens when we die has preoccupied people throughout history. Different religions attempt to answer this question in different ways. Muslims believe that human life is a gift from God, but also a test. They believe that when people die they wait in their graves until the **Day of Judgement**. On this day, God will judge all people who have ever lived and decide what happens to them in the afterlife. Muslims believe that, while people wait in their graves, God sends two angels to ask them about their beliefs and how they have lived. If people answer correctly, then they have a peaceful experience in the grave. If they answer incorrectly, they are tormented until the Day of Judgement.

Those who have fully submitted themselves to God will be rewarded with **Jannah** (paradise, heaven). Muslims believe that Jannah is beyond what humans can imagine, but the Qur'an likens it to a beautiful garden with four rivers of water, milk, honey and wine running through it. Nobody in Jannah will experience suffering. It will be a place of complete comfort and contentment, and people will never grow tired of it. In order to enter Jannah, people will have to cross a bridge. This will be easy for those who are destined for heaven, but those who are not will fall from the bridge and face terrible torments in the fires of **Jahannam** (hell).

Islamic artwork from the 14th century showing a paradise garden with a refreshing stream, flowering trees and birds.

Muslims believe that God wants everyone to enter Jannah, but people must choose whether to believe in one God, to accept the teachings of the Qur'an and to perform good acts, such as giving money to charity.

Muslims interpret the Qur'an's vivid descriptions of heaven and hell in different ways. Some think that the Qur'an should be understood literally. However, others think that it contains metaphors to describe a reality for which we do not have words. Non-Muslims might argue that the descriptions were simply to encourage people at the time of Muhammad to follow Islam through either fear of hell or the promise of many rewards in heaven. For example, the image of four rivers would have appealed to people living in a hot desert environment.

Hell and the Tree of Zaqqum

According to the Qur'an, the Tree of Zaqqum grows from the fire at the bottom of hell and its flowers are the heads of devils. Those in hell must eat the fruit of the tree, which makes their insides burn. The fires of hell are kept alight by burning bodies. When someone's skin is burned up, he or she is given new skin, which is then burned afresh. This happens for all eternity. The flames are hotter than any flame on earth and people will be in continual pain and misery.

An artist's depiction of the Tree of Zaqqum.

The Six Articles of Faith

Most Muslims think that getting to Jannah requires a mixture of good deeds and faith. Sunni Muslims believe that when Muhammad was asked about faith, he said that it involved six things. These are known as the Six Articles of Faith. They are:

- belief in God

- belief in angels

- belief in God's books (the Qur'an and other holy writings, some of which have been lost)

- belief in God's prophets

- belief in the Day of Judgement

- belief in God's plan.

> 66 Those who believe and do good deeds will have an unfailing reward. 99
>
> Qur'an 95:6–7

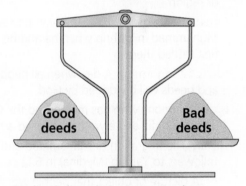

Muslims believe that everyone's actions will be weighed on the Day of Judgement.

The Day of Judgement

On the Day of Judgement, Muslims believe that all people will be judged on whether they have had faith and whether they have done good things on earth. Everyone is responsible for himself or herself and the actions of each person are weighed in a divine balance. Only God knows the minimum weight required to get into heaven, but good deeds count 10 times more than bad. Many Muslims do not think that all people in hell will be destined to remain there forever; because God is merciful, some people might enter heaven after being in hell.

Key vocabulary

Day of Judgement A day when all people's faith and deeds will be judged by God

Jahannam Hell

Jannah Paradise or heaven

Check your understanding

1 What do Muslims believe will happen on the Day of Judgement?

2 What are the Six Articles of Faith?

3 How does the Qur'an describe Jannah and Jahannam?

4 Explain how different Muslims might interpret the Qur'an's descriptions of Jannah and Jahannam.

5 'There is no life after death.' Discuss this statement, with reference to Islam.

Unit 1: History and belief
Knowledge organiser

Key vocabulary

99 names of God 99 characteristics of God used by Muslims to try to describe what God is like

Allah The Arabic word for God

caliph The Arabic word for the leader of the whole Muslim community after the death of Muhammad; it literally means 'successor'. Sunni Muslims call the first four caliphs 'Rightly Guided Caliphs'

Caliphate The Islamic community ruled over by the caliph

circumcise To remove a male's foreskin

civil war A war between people of the same nation or region

Constitution of Medina The laws passed by Muhammad in Yathrib when he and his followers first settled there

Day of Judgement A day when all people's faith and deeds will be judged by God

hafiz Someone who has memorised the Qur'an (a man is a hafiz and a woman is called a hafiza)

Hijrah The migration of Muhammad and his followers to Yathrib (Medina) in 622 CE

idol A picture or object that people worship as part of their religion

Jahannam Hell

Jannah Paradise or heaven

Ka'aba A key holy site in Mecca; before Muhammad's time, this building contained 360 idols

Mecca A city in present-day Saudi Arabia; Muhammad was born here in 570 CE

Medina One of the main cities in Arabia in the time of Muhammad (originally called Yathrib); Muhammad and his followers fled here to escape persecution and create a new Muslim community

monotheism Belief in one God

mosque The place of worship for Muslims; it literally means 'place of prostration'

polytheism Belief in many gods

prophet A messenger of God

Qur'an The holy book of Islam, which Muslims believe contains the word of God; it literally means 'recitation'

Ramadan The ninth month of the Islamic year (which is based on the moon)

Revelation A message revealed by God to humans

Shi'a A minority group of Muslims who believe that Ali and his descendants should have succeeded Muhammad as leaders of Islam; the word means 'party of Ali'

shirk The Arabic word for the sin of worshipping anything other than God

Sunni The majority (about 85 per cent) of Muslims across the world who believe that the Rightly Guided Caliphs were rightful successors of Muhammad; the word means 'people of the tradition'

surah A chapter of the Qur'an; there are 114 surahs in total

tawhid Belief in the oneness of God

The Blue Mosque, Istanbul, Turkey.

Key facts

- Islam is the second-largest and fastest-growing religion in the world. It is a monotheistic faith that began in Arabia in the lifetime of the Prophet Muhammad, who was born in Mecca in 570 CE. Islam means 'submission' and Muslim means 'one who submits to God'.

- Muslims believe that Muhammad received revelations over 23 years from God about how people should live. The first revelation was received from the angel Jibril in 610 CE while Muhammad was praying in a cave. This event is known as the Night of Power. The revelations received by Muhammad were memorised by his followers and recorded in a book called the Qur'an after his death.

- Muhammad was a religious and political leader as well as a warrior who ruled first over Medina and then Mecca. He fought against persecution of early Muslims and by the end of his life was the most influential man in the Arabian Peninsula. He gained wide recognition as a prophet and brought previously warring tribes under Islamic rule.

- After Muhammad's death, Islam continued to spread under the rule of the caliphs, and a large Caliphate (empire) was established. However, there was disagreement amongst Muslims over who should succeed Muhammad as leader, which caused the religion to split into two groups: Sunni Muslims and Shi'a Muslims.

- Modern versions of the Qur'an are based on an official Qur'an compiled under the rule of the third caliph, Uthman. The Qur'an is written in Arabic and split into 114 surahs. It is believed to be the word of God and is treated with great respect by Muslims.

- Tawhid – the belief that God is one – is the most important Islamic belief. Anything that goes against tawhid is considered shirk. Muslims often describe God using 99 names, but ultimately Muslims believe that God is beyond anything that humans can describe or imagine.

- Muslims believe that Muhammad was the final prophet sent by God, but they believe God also revealed himself to earlier prophets mentioned in Jewish and Christian scriptures, like Adam, Abraham and Moses. Muslims believe that Jesus was a prophet, but think that viewing him as the Son of God is shirk.

- Muslims believe that there will be a Day of Judgement, when God will send people to paradise (Jannah) or hell (Jahannam) depending on their faith and deeds.

Key people

Abu Bakr The first Rightly Guided Caliph (632–634 CE) and Muhammad's closest companion

Abu Talib Muhammad's uncle

Ali The fourth Rightly Guided Caliph (656–661 CE) and Muhammad's cousin and son-in-law

Amina Muhammad's mother

Bilal A former slave who was one of Islam's first converts

Fatima Muhammad's daughter, who married Ali

Hussein Ali's son, who was killed in the Battle of Karbala

Ibrahim A prophet in Islam, known as Abraham in English.

Isa An important prophet in Islam; Jesus in English

Khadija A wealthy businesswoman and widow who became Muhammad's wife when she was 40 and was also the first to believe his message after the Night of Power

Muawiya The successor to Ali as the fifth caliph

Muhammad The final prophet, who received God's full revelation; he lived from 570–632 CE; Muslims will say or write PBUH after his name to show respect

Musa An important prophet in Islam; in English, Moses

Umar The second Rightly Guided Caliph (634–644 CE)

Uthman The third Rightly Guided Caliph (644–656 CE)

Islam in the modern world

In this book's second part, you will find out about how Muslims practise their religion in the modern world. You will explore the Five Pillars, which are central to life as a Muslim, and consider the challenges that Muslims face when following these today. You will also consider some of the most controversial questions people ask about Islam. Should women cover their bodies and faces? What is jihad? What is Islamophobia?

2

The Five Pillars

What five practices are central to life as a Muslim?

In most religions, faith must be matched with action. It is not good enough just to know what the right thing to do is – you have to actually *do* it. Islam is no exception. The **Five Pillars** are five acts of worship that all Muslims are expected to do in their lives, if it is possible. They are called pillars because they help support a Muslim's faith; therefore, if one of the pillars collapses, his or her whole faith may fall with it. Sunni and Shi'a Muslims generally agree on the importance of these five acts.

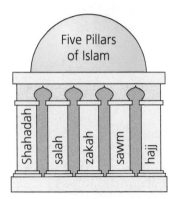
The Five Pillars of Islam.

1. The Shahadah (declaration of faith)

The **Shahadah** is the declaration of faith that there is only one God and that Muhammad is his messenger. This belief in the oneness of God (tawhid) is at the heart of Islam and was the reason why Muhammad and his followers were persecuted in its early years. The Shahadah is always recited in Arabic, the language of the Qur'an. A Muslim will say it thousands of time over the course of his or her lifetime as part of prayer. It is also whispered into the ears of children at birth and of Muslims at death.

> **The Shahadah**
> 66 La ilaha illa Allah, Muhammad rasul Allah. 99
> This translate as: 'There is no god but God, and Muhammad is his messenger.'

Fact

Shi'a Muslims add Arabic words meaning 'Ali is the friend (*wali*) of God' to the first two parts of the Shahadah.

2. Salah (prayer)

The Arabic word '**salah**' is usually translated as 'prayer', but it can also mean 'worship'. The Qur'an only mentions praying three times a day, but most Muslims pray five times. Muslims are not restricted to praying five times a day – they can pray to God anywhere at any time, for example, to ask God for help or to give him thanks. When praying informally, prayers are usually said in the language of the person praying rather than in Arabic.

3. Zakah (charity)

Each year, a Muslim must give 2.5 per cent of his or her savings to charity. This is called **zakah**. Muslims believe that their wealth is given to them by God and they therefore have a responsibility to share some of it with those who are less fortunate than themselves. 'Zakah' literally means 'that which purifies'. Muslims believe that zakah purifies the remainder of their money and prevents them from becoming greedy.

A Muslim woman praying.

4. Sawm (fasting during Ramadan)

'**Sawm**' is the Arabic term for fasting during the month of Ramadan, when the fast lasts from dawn to sunset. All Muslims are encouraged to fast, except those who are very young, very old, or who cannot fast for health reasons or other circumstances, such as travelling or being pregnant.

There are many spiritual benefits to fasting. Muslims feel a strong sense of the global Muslim community, the **ummah**, because everyone is fasting at the same time, and it helps them to consider the challenges faced by the poor. It is an extra test of self-control for Muslims living in Britain – unlike in Middle Eastern countries, the majority of the population is *not* fasting. A celebratory meal is often shared in the evenings, when the fast is over.

5. Hajj (pilgrimage to Mecca)

Every Muslim hopes that at some point in life he or she can make a **pilgrimage** to Mecca. This pilgrimage is called **hajj**. Each year, in the 12th month of the Islamic calendar, about three million pilgrims set off from different parts of the globe to reach Mecca and participate in the most spiritual of all journeys for a Muslim. It is a Muslim's duty to make this pilgrimage at least once, if they are physically able and wealthy enough to do so. Like fasting during Ramadan, Muslims think that the shared experience of hajj strengthens the ummah, as well as their own faith.

Millions of pilgrims visit the Ka'aba in Mecca every year.

Key vocabulary

Five Pillars Five important acts of worship in a Muslim's life, which form the basis of the faith

hajj A pilgrimage to Mecca

pilgrimage A journey taken to a place of religious importance

salah Prayers that Muslims must perform five times a day

sawm Fasting during the month of Ramadan

Shahadah The Muslim declaration of faith – there is no god but God, and Muhammad is his messenger

ummah The global community of Muslims

zakah The act of giving 2.5 per cent of your savings to charity

Fact

Before the invention of aeroplanes, many pilgrims would travel for years by foot or camel across Africa or Asia to reach Mecca. They would be greatly respected for doing so, and this achievement of completing hajj would be recognised by people gaining the status of hajji (a man) or hajja (a woman).

Check your understanding

1 What are the names of the Five Pillars of Islam?

2 How often do Muslims pray?

3 Which of the Five Pillars means literally 'that which purifies'? Why is this pillar important?

4 What do Muslims believe are the benefits of fasting?

5 Why do you think the Shahadah is the most important of the Five Pillars for Muslims?

Prayer and the mosque

How do Muslims pray, and what happens in a mosque?

The Shahadah (declaration of faith) is the most important of the Five Pillars. The second most important is salah – prayer five times a day. Salah provides an opportunity for Muslims to show submission – 'islam' to God. Prayers are always said in Arabic and usually happen at dawn, midday, mid-afternoon, dusk and evening. Prayers can be performed in any location, but whenever possible many Muslims choose to attend a mosque where the prayers are led by an imam (leader). The imam stands in front of others with his back to them while leading the prayers.

The only time when attending mosque is compulsory is for Friday noon prayers, and this only applies to men. Women are not required to attend, but if they do, they pray in a separate part of the mosque or behind the men. This is so that men are not distracted during prayer. On a Friday, the imam will deliver a sermon.

The five times a day when Muslims should pray are announced by a **muezzin** reciting the **adhan** (call to prayer). The muezzin can do this inside the mosque or from one of the mosque's towers, known as **minarets**. The adhan reminds Muslims of the key beliefs of Islam – there is no god but God, and Muhammad is his messenger.

A muezzin calling Muslims to prayer. Today, speakers are often used so that the adhan can be better heard.

Wudu

Before praying, Muslims must perform a ritual wash known as **wudu** . This involves washing hands, mouth, nostrils, face, arms, the top of the head and feet a specific number of times in a particular order. Most

---

The adhan (call to prayer)
❝ *Allahu akbar Allahu akbar* [said twice]
God is the greatest, God is the greatest
Ashhadu an lailaha illAllah [said twice]
I bear witness that there is no God but God
Ashhadu anna Muhammadan rasul Allah [said twice]
I bear witness that Muhammad is the Messenger of God
Hayya aala as-salah, hayya aala as-salah
Come to prayer, come to prayer
Hayya aala al-falah, hayya aala al-falah
Come to success, come to success
Allahu akbar, Allahu akbar
God is the greatest, God is the greatest
La ilaha illAllah
There is no God but God ❞

Activity

Listen to a call to prayer and see if you can follow the Arabic in the purple box below.

Fact

When entering a mosque, Muslims remove their shoes to show respect to God and keep the space clean. When Muslims perform salah outside of a mosque, they pray on a prayer mat to make sure that they are still praying somewhere clean. They will also remove their shoes before standing on the mat.

mosques have an area where people can perform this ritual. There are usually separate areas for men and women.

After washing, the person is ready to pray. This is done in the main prayer hall, which is found in all mosques. The word 'mosque' literally means 'place of prostration'. Unlike many other religious buildings, the main prayer room in a mosque does not contain seats, because Muslims need space to pray. As they pray, people perform a series of movements – for example, standing, bowing and **prostrating**.

When praying together, Muslims stand shoulder to shoulder to show that they are united and equal as part of the ummah. In mosques, there is usually an alcove in a wall called a **mihrab**, which points towards Mecca. Muslims always face in the direction of Mecca when they pray.

What do mosques look like?

As well as having minarets, it is common for mosques to have a dome. There are practical and religious reasons for this. In hot countries, the dome helps to keep the mosque cool. It also amplifies sound. However, it is also symbolic of God's rule over everything and of the worldwide ummah. The only piece of furniture normally found inside the prayer room of a mosque is a platform called a **minbar**. This is where the imam delivers his sermon.

There are approximately 1750 mosques in the UK today, but it is not always easy to spot them from the outside. This is because there is a mix of purpose-built mosques and houses, churches and other buildings that have been converted into mosques.

During prayer, Muslims perform a series of movements (rak'ah).

Some of the most architecturally impressive buildings in the world are mosques.

Fact

As well as a place to pray, Mosques are used as Madrassahs – places for children to learn Arabic and how to pray, and to memorise the Qur'an.

Activity

Imagine you have visited a mosque. Using all the key words on this page, write a diary entry explaining what you saw and why it was happening.

Key vocabulary

adhan The call to prayer

mihrab An alcove in a mosque wall showing the direction of Mecca

minaret A mosque tower on a mosque from which the muezzin traditionally gives the adhan

minbar A platform in a mosque from which the imam delivers his sermon

muezzin A person responsible for performing the adhan in a mosque

prostrating Bowing with part of the body above the knees touching the floor, such as the hands

wudu Ritual washing before prayer

Check your understanding

1 Why is prayer important to Muslims, and when and where is it done?

2 What is the role of the muezzin and the adhan?

3 What is wudu?

4 How do Muslims perform salah?

5 Describe the features that mosques often have in common.

Unit 2: Islam in the modern world
Ramadan and Eid ul-Fitr

Why do Muslims fast during Ramadan, and what happens at Eid ul-Fitr?

What is Ramadan?

During the month of Ramadan, Muslims celebrate Muhammad receiving his first revelation from the angel Jibril on the Night of Power. This is believed to have happened towards the end of Ramadan. On this night, Muslims will often stay awake praying, as they believe that God is particularly merciful at this time.

Each year, during the 30 days of Ramadan, Muslims will not eat or drink between sunrise and sunset. This is called sawm – fasting – and is the fourth pillar of Islam. Fasting during this month is commanded in the Qur'an. Muslims think that fasting can provide spiritual strength and self-control over greed and other selfish instincts. It also helps develop compassion for people who are living in poverty, without enough food and drink, and helps increase people's gratitude for what they have. Last, Muslims believe that the fast helps strengthen the global community of Muslims, the ummah, because all Muslims are sharing in the same experience.

Not every Muslim is required to fast during Ramadan. People who are ill, pregnant, elderly or young (usually under about 12 years old) are not expected to fast. Soldiers and people who are travelling on long journeys are also permitted to miss the fast, but should make up the missed days at another time.

Muslims believe that if they do not live in a way that honours God during Ramadan, then their fast has no spiritual value. Muhammad is reported to have said: 'There are many who fast during the day and pray all night, but they gain nothing but hunger and sleeplessness.' As well as paying special attention to the way they treat others, Muslims might read the Qur'an or attend mosque more often during this month.

Ramadan is the ninth month of the Islamic year, which is based on the moon. This means that every year Ramadan occurs about 11 days earlier than the previous year. As such, the number of hours that Muslims are required to fast can vary greatly. In the summer months, the fast lasts longer than the winter months, when there are fewer hours of daylight. Going without food and water in the heat of summer can be especially difficult.

At the end each day of fasting, people may enjoy a large meal and celebrate the achievement of completing the fast. Often, families will also share a pre-fast meal together early in the morning before the fast begins. In the summer, there is not as long between the evening and morning meals, so the morning meal is quite light. In winter, the morning meal is eaten later, and so is generally more substantial.

> ### Fact
> Nothing is allowed to enter people's mouths while fasting. This means that people cannot smoke or chew gum. Even swallowing water while swimming is seen as breaking the fast.

The fast is usually broken by eating a date, as it is believed that this is how Muhammad broke his fast.

Eid ul-Fitr

Ramadan ends with a three-day celebration known as **Eid ul-Fitr**, which begins on the first day of the 10th month of the year. Usually, on the first day of Eid ul-Fitr, Muslim families attend mosque to thank God that their fast is complete. They are reminded by the imam that Muhammad promised that those who complete the fast will receive both pleasure on earth and also a reward from God on the Day of Judgement.

Festivities to celebrate Eid ul-Fitr.

Eid ul-Fitr is a time of both prayer and celebration. Muslims will often decorate their houses, eat feasts together and give each other gifts and cards. It is also a popular time for Muslims to get married. In Muslim-majority countries, Eid is a public holiday like Christmas and Easter are in the UK. In countries where Islam is not the majority religion, Muslims will usually take time off work in order to celebrate Eid. Some employers may give Muslim employees a day off work.

Eid ul-Adha

During the 12th month of the Islamic year, Muslims have another celebration, called **Eid ul-Adha**, when the prophet Abraham's faith and obedience to God are remembered. Eid ul-Adha takes place at the end of the five days of hajj, but is celebrated by Muslims all around the world.

A carnival in Morocco to celebrate Eid ul-Adha.

Key vocabulary

Eid ul-Adha A four-day celebration in the final 12 month of the Islamic year

Eid ul-Fitr A three-day celebration after Ramadan

Check your understanding

1. What must Muslims do and not do during Ramadan?
2. Name three groups of people who do not have to fast.
3. Why do Muslims fast during Ramadan?
4. How are the dates of Ramadan decided and how does this affect those fasting?
5. Describe what happens at the end of the month of Ramadan.

Unit 2: Islam in the modern world
What happens on hajj?

Hajj is a pilgrimage that every Muslim tries to undertake during the course of his or her lifetime, but what does this physical and spiritual journey involve?

Muhammad lived on the Arabian Peninsula, and this is where Muslims believe that he received the Qur'an. As you have seen, the city of Mecca has great significance in Islam, and it is here – and places nearby – that the Qur'an tells Muslims to visit. They must do this on a pilgrimage called hajj at least once in their life, if they are able.

In order for the pilgrimage to have spiritual value, pilgrims must not be in debt and must make sure their family is provided for while they are away. Certain people are not required to go on hajj – for example, people who are too old, poor or ill. One person can also go on hajj on behalf of others. The pilgrimage has to take place from 8 to 12 Dhul-Hijjah, the final month of the Islamic calendar. There are approximately three million pilgrims in Mecca during hajj.

The prophet's mosque

Before arriving in Mecca, many pilgrims visit the Prophet's Mosque in Medina to prepare themselves spiritually for hajj by praying. The mosque can hold almost 700,000 people. It contains the tomb of Muhammad and the first two caliphs, and is the second holiest site in the world for Muslims. Some Muslims choose to travel to Medina after, rather than before, completing hajj.

The Prophet's Mosque in Medina.

Ihram

When approaching Mecca, pilgrims must enter into a spiritual state of holiness or purity known as **ihram**. While in this state, pilgrims are not allowed to do various things, including smoke, shave, wear perfume or jewellery, or cut their nails. It is a time to focus wholly on God. At this time, all pilgrims wear the same white cotton clothing. Men usually wear one cotton sheet around their waist and one over their shoulder. Women wear a long white dress and head covering and do not cover their faces. The simple clothing worn by pilgrims is intended to show purity and humility before God, as well as equality between all people on hajj. It is also a reminder to pilgrims to focus on God rather than their everyday lives.

What happens in Mecca?

During hajj, some pilgrims stay in hotels, many stay in tents and others may simply sleep on roadsides. There are various tasks to be completed within the five days. With the high temperatures and with so many people in one place all trying to do the same things, this can be a challenge.

The simple clothing people wear in the state of ihram is a reminder to focus on God rather than everyday life.

On arriving in Mecca, pilgrims head towards the Grand Mosque, which is home to the Ka'aba. Pilgrims walk around the Ka'aba seven times in an anticlockwise direction. Those who can get close enough might try to touch or kiss it, but the mosque can hold millions of people and so not everyone has this opportunity.

After circling the Ka'aba, pilgrims walk or run back and forth between two hills, Marwah and Safa. Muslims believe that Abraham's wife rushed between these two hills in search of water for her dehydrated son, Ishmael. Travelling between the hills also symbolises the desperate search of the pilgrims' souls to find God. In the past, this took place outdoors, but now there are two long air-conditioned corridors.

The stages of hajj.

During hajj, pilgrims stand on or near Mount Arafat from noon to sunset, praying for forgiveness from God. This is a significant location, because it is believed to be where God forgave Adam and Eve after they disobeyed him by eating fruit from a tree that was forbidden to them, and also where Muhammad delivered his final sermon. Many pilgrims describe a feeling of freedom and joy as they receive God's forgiveness for everything they have done wrong.

After Mount Arafat, pilgrims collect stones and head to Mina to throw the stones at three pillars, which represent Satan. This is done to remember the willingness of the prophet Abraham to sacrifice his son, Ishmael, despite Satan telling him not to. It also symbolises Muslims' own rejection of evil. The stoning of Satan is often followed by the open-air sacrifice of an animal such as a goat or sheep. The meat can be eaten in Mina, but is often frozen and sent to poor Muslims in other countries.

At the end of hajj, pilgrims leave the state of ihram, and men will join a queue outside one of Mecca's many barber shops to have their heads shaved. Women usually just have one lock of their hair removed. Finally, pilgrims complete their pilgrimage by returning to the Ka'aba and circling it seven more times.

Fact

In 2015, it is estimated that approximately 2000 people died in a stampede while throwing stones at Satan. In response to this tragedy, all pilgrims were given electronic GPS bracelets to wear in 2016, and 1000 cameras were installed at holy sites to alert organisers of overcrowding.

Activity

Write a travel guide for hajj, giving advice on how to prepare, what will happen and why, and explaining what Muslims believe are the benefits of this pilgrimage.

Key vocabulary

ihram The state of holiness or purity entered into by pilgrims before beginning hajj

Check your understanding

1 Who is and who is not required to go on hajj?
2 When does hajj take place and how might a Muslim prepare for it?
3 Explain what Muslims do and do not do while in the state of ihram and why.
4 Describe what happens on hajj and explain why these things are done.
5 'All religious people should go on pilgrimage.' Discuss this statement.

Unit 2: Islam in the modern world
Sunni and Shi'a Islam

What are the similarities and differences between Sunni and Shi'a Muslims, and what effect does this have in the modern world?

Similarities

Today, the majority of Muslims – about 85 per cent – are Sunni. In Britain, approximately 95 per cent of Muslims are Sunni. Although Sunni and Shi'a Muslims disagree over who should have succeeded Muhammad (see pages 14–15), there is much that they do agree on. Both groups believe that there is only one God and that Muhammad was his final prophet. They both use the Qur'an as the basis of their beliefs and they both follow the Five Pillars, although Shi'a Muslims have other practices that they believe are similarly important. Both Sunni and Shi'a Muslims attend mosque to pray at noon on a Friday, although they use a slightly different adhan and different prayer positions. The Qur'an only specifies praying three times a day, so some Shi'a Muslims combine the five daily prayers into three sets of prayers.

When Muslims first moved to Britain, Sunni and Shi'a Muslims would often share the same places to pray, but as Islam grew in Britain this became less common and the different branches of Islam developed their own identities.

> **Fact**
>
> The largest form of Shi'a Islam is known as Twelver Shi'a, but there are other types of Shi'a Islam: the Isma'ilis (Seveners) and the Zaydis (Fivers). These groups are given their names because of their differing beliefs about how many imams followed Muhammad.

Differences

Sunni Muslims believe that the Qur'an, **Hadith** (the reported teachings of Muhammad) and Sunnah (the example of Muhammad) show them how to live. These three sources form the basis of **Shari'a law**, which provides guidance on all aspects of life.

Shi'a Muslims believe that God did not want to leave his people without a spiritual leader on earth, so he chose 12 **imams** – Ali and his descendants. God gave the imams the ability to be examples for Muslims, leading them in all aspects of life and showing them the truth that they should follow. Shi'a Muslims believe that in 874 CE, when the 12th imam was six years old, God took him into hiding to avoid him being killed as the previous imams had been. They think that he will return at the end of time, along with Jesus, to bring peace and justice to earth.

The site of a suicide car bomb in Karbala, Iraq, during a Shi'a pilgrimage.

Both Sunni and Shi'a Muslims celebrate Ramadan, Eid ul-Fitr and Eid ul-Adha, but they remember different events during the Islamic festival of Ashura.

Iraqi Shi'a men beating themselves with chains to remember the assassination of Ali's son, Hussein.

Sunni Muslims remember the prophet Noah leaving the ark and Moses being freed from the Egyptians, while Shi'a Muslims mourn the death of Ali's son Hussein, who was beheaded during the Battle of Karbala (in present-day Iraq). During this festival, Shi'as often wear dark clothes, blacken their faces and bodies, and beat their chests with their fists to show their sorrow. In countries such as Pakistan and India, some men even cut themselves with knives, chains and blades to draw blood and suffer as Hussein did.

Shari'a Law

Shari'a Law teaches Muslims what is **halal**. '*Halal*' is an Arabic word meaning 'permitted'. The word is most often heard when describing food, but it can also be used to describe prayer, fasting, clothes or other things – any object or action can be halal. The opposite of halal is **haram**, which means 'unlawful' or 'forbidden'. Any meat that Muslims eat must be halal. For meat to be halal, the animal needs to be killed by cutting the jugular vein, carotid artery and windpipe with a sharp knife. All blood is then drained from the animal. During this process, an Islamic blessing is recited. Muslims believe that eating pork and drinking alcohol is always haram.

There are many halal butchers and restaurants in the UK.

Modern clashes

Many Muslims accept that both Sunni and Shi'a Islam are valid forms of their religion, but there have been conflicts between the two groups, which continue today. There are many reasons for clashes between Sunnis and Shi'as. In Iraq, there has been much violence between Sunni and Shi'a Muslims caused by historical, religious and political factors. For example, in 2007, at a popular time of Shi'a pilgrimage to Karbala in Iraq, a car bomb was set off near a Shi'a mosque. Approximately 60 people were killed and about 150 more were injured. Violence erupted on the streets and there were many shootings.

Key vocabulary

Ashura A festival in which Shi'a Muslims mourn the death of Ali's son Hussein at the Battle of Karbala

Hadith The reported sayings of Muhammad, heard by people during his life and written down in the centuries after his death

halal Permitted

haram Forbidden

imam A word used by Shi'a Muslims to refer to Ali and his 11 descendants. It also means the leader of prayers in a Sunni mosque

Shari'a law Guidance on all aspects of life for Muslims, from the three main sources of authority – the Qur'an, Sunnah and Hadith

Check your understanding

1 Which is the largest branch of Islam in the world?

2 In a table, show the similarities and differences between Sunni and Shi'a Muslims.

3 Explain what is meant by Shar'ia Law and how it helps Muslims?

4 What is halal food?

5 Explain the significance of the festival of Ashura to different Muslims.

What should women wear?

Why does the issue of what Muslim women wear cause controversy amongst both Muslims and non-Muslims?

The Qur'an teaches that both men and women should dress modestly. This is interpreted in different ways by different Muslims. Some believe it means that women should wear a **hijab** – a scarf that covers some or all of the head. Other Muslims believe that dressing modestly means wearing a **niqab** – a cloth that covers the whole face except the eyes. There are also Muslims who believe that to dress modestly means women wearing a **burqa** – a garment that covers the body from head to toe, often with a mesh screen to see through. In most Islamic countries, the hijab is considered sufficient. However, there are also Muslims who choose not to wear any religious covering at all.

Recently, some European countries have banned Muslim women from wearing religious coverings in public. This has caused much controversy. Some of the arguments that are made by both sides are explained below. Some people believe that all religious coverings are wrong, while others are just against the niqab or burqa, but not the hijab.

Arguments for banning coverings

Those who do not support women wearing a covering sometimes claim that women are forced to wear these garments by their husbands or fathers against their own will. This is considered oppressive and as evidence that women are seen as inferior by male Muslims. People argue that wearing a covering belongs to a different time, when people had different views from those found in modern Europe. They say that we now live in more forward-looking and **secular** societies.

Some people also argue that wearing a covering like the niqab stops Muslim women from integrating into European societies. They see it as a sign of separation that sends a message to non-Muslims that they are different. This makes it more difficult for Muslims and non-Muslims to have a positive relationship. Some people simply say that they think covering the head or body is impolite or that it frightens them in some way.

Sometimes the media have used images of women wearing a niqab when reporting on acts of terrorism carried out by other people claiming to be Muslims. Some newspapers have done this when the act was not carried out by people wearing any covering. This sort of treatment of Islam may make people link the idea of covering one's body with terrorism, so they feel threatened by it.

Arguments against banning coverings

On the other hand, many Muslim women say that covering their hair, face or body is something that they have chosen to do – men have not made them do so. They argue that religious freedom means women have the right to wear a covering if they choose.

> **Fact**
>
> Most Muslims think that men should be covered from the navel to the knees, but there are also countries where it would be considered immodest for a man to wear shorts and show his bare legs.

A woman wearing a hijab.

A woman wearing a niqab.

A woman wearing a burqa.

Some Muslim women argue that wearing a covering maintains their dignity; it allows them to be respected. It stops them from being simply an object to which men are attracted. It focuses men's attention on what is most important – the quality of a woman's character – rather than external beauty. They say that real freedom and equality means making it possible for women to be respected while covering themselves. Coverings, they may argue, also free women from having to spend time making themselves look a certain way in an attempt to meet the expectations of what society says is attractive.

Some people argue that wearing a covering does not encourage separation between Muslims and non-Muslims. Rather, it gives freedom to Muslim women to take part in society without compromising their beliefs or abandoning their identity as a Muslim, which could cause them to lose the respect of others in their community. An example of this is wearing a **burkini**.

A burkini is a type of swimsuit that covers most of the body. In 2016, it was banned in some places in France, and women who continued to wear it were fined.

Feminist attitudes

Some **feminists** are critical of what they see as **patriarchal** attitudes in Muslim-majority countries in parts of the Middle East. For example, in Saudi Arabia, women can be punished for not covering their heads and bodies. It is also illegal for women to drive in Saudi Arabia. Feminists also criticise the practice of polygamy (men having more than one wife), which is legal in some Islamic countries. The Qur'an permits a man to have up to four wives if he can treat each wife equally. Like many Arabian men of his time, Muhammad is thought to have had 12 wives, including Khadija. However, many people believe that this is an outdated and unfair practice that should not be permitted in the modern world.

Key vocabulary

burkini Swimwear worn by Muslim women to maintain modesty; it was banned in 20 French towns in 2016

burqa A cloak that covers the body from head to toe, often with a mesh screen to see through

feminist Someone who argues for women's rights and believes women are not being treated equally

hijab A scarf that covers some or all of the head and hair, but not the face

niqab A cloth that covers the head and face, except the eyes

patriarchal A word used to describe a society where men have more power and control than women

secular Non-religious

Check your understanding

1. What does the Qur'an teach about how Muslims should dress?
2. What is the difference between a hijab, niqab and burqa?
3. Explain two arguments for, and two arguments against, banning religious coverings.
4. Explain why feminists might be critical of what happens in some Islamic countries.
5. 'Religious clothing should not be worn publicly in the UK.' Discuss this statement.

What is jihad?

The Arabic word '*jihad*' literally means 'to struggle' and can refer to a physical or a spiritual struggle. How has jihad been interpreted and carried out throughout the centuries?

Lesser jihad

In the years following the Night of Power, Muhammad and his followers were persecuted because of their monotheistic message. The polytheistic tribes who lived in Mecca, including the Quraysh tribe, used violence to prevent Muhammad from preaching. As a result, Muhammad and his followers fled from Mecca to Medina, where they established the first Islamic community.

While in Medina, the Qur'an continued to be revealed to Muhammad. The revelations he received included practical matters, such as how the new community should work and what laws its people should follow. As Muhammad was establishing his new community in Medina, he and his followers were attacked. The revelations received during this time explained when fighting should and should not happen.

> **❝** They ask you [Prophet] about fighting in the sacred month. Say, 'Fighting in that month is a great offence, but to bar others from God's path, to disbelieve in Him, prevent access to the Sacred Mosque, and expel its people, are still greater offences in God's eyes: persecution is worse than killing.' **❞**
>
> Qur'an 2:217

Muslims believe that passages of the Qur'an such as the one above show that fighting was an acceptable means of self-defence for the early Muslim community in Medina. Islam could have been wiped out if Muhammad and his persecuted followers did not fight in order to preserve their religion. However, Muhammad and his followers did not just fight in self-defence – they also fought to help spread the message of Islam. It was not unusual to go to war in order to gain power at this time. The Mesopotamians, Greeks and Romans all fought against others to extend their political power.

By the time of Muhammad's death, Muslims had conquered the whole of Arabia, and within a century of his death Muhammad's followers had carried his message to Syria, Iraq, Jerusalem and further west into Egypt and North Africa, establishing a large Islamic Caliphate or empire. By 750 CE, the Caliphate stretched from the westernmost point of Spain to the western edge of India.

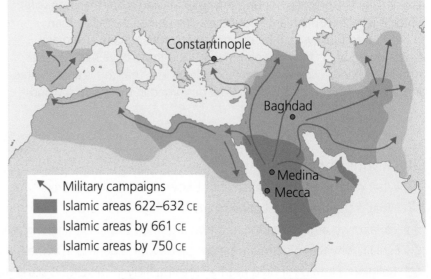

Military campaigns
Islamic areas 622–632 CE
Islamic areas by 661 CE
Islamic areas by 750 CE

A map showing some of the areas under Islamic rule by 750 CE.

Islamic militancy today

The majority of people today believe that people should be free to choose their religion (or no religion), rather than having a particular religion forced upon them. The majority of Muslims also believe that using violence to spread Islam is unacceptable. However, groups of Islamic **militants** such as Al-Qaeda, Boko Haram and Islamic State in Iraq and Syria (also called ISIS or Daesh) disagree. They believe Jews, Christians and other Muslims are guilty of shirk and use the Arabic word *'kafir'* to identify them as 'unbelievers' who need to be killed. Such groups want to set up an Islamic Caliphate in Syria and Iraq, free from what they see as 'impure' Western influences.

Muslims protesting against the use of their religion to justify acts of terrorism.

On 11 September 2001, two aeroplanes were hijacked by Al-Qaeda and flown into the World Trade Center in New York, killing nearly 3000 people. Since then, there have been many more terrorist attacks by Islamic militants, including bombings in London in 2005 and Paris in 2015. The vast majority of Muslims are appalled by the actions of these groups and reject both their violent interpretation of the Qur'an and also their attitude towards people of different religions.

Greater jihad

Most Muslims today interpret jihad as either a spiritual struggle inside oneself or as a fight against injustice rather than a physical struggle against an enemy. They point to a difference in what they call 'lesser jihad' and 'greater jihad'. Lesser jihad is the physical struggle to defend Islam. The *greater* jihad is to struggle against unfairness in the world and selfish desires within everyone, by following the teachings of Muhammad. An example of this struggle might be fasting during the month of Ramadan, saving money to give to the poor or speaking out against unfairness in the world.

Key vocabulary

jihad Literally, 'struggle'; this can be physical or spiritual

militants Individuals or groups who use violence to spread their ideas

Check your understanding

❶ Why were Muhammad and the early Muslims persecuted?

❷ Why did Muhammad and the early Muslims fight?

❸ Explain what Islamic militant groups believe.

❹ What do the majority of Muslims think about the views and actions of Islamic militants?

❺ Using examples, explain what is meant by 'lesser' and 'greater' jihad.

Islam in Britain

Muslims make up approximately 5 per cent of the total population of Britain today. When did Muslims start living in Britain and what is life like for them today?

Islam arrives in Britain

When the Second World War ended in 1945, Britain ruled over a large empire that included the countries we now call India, Pakistan and Bangladesh. The British government invited people living in the empire to move to Britain in order to help rebuild the country. Many Muslims in Britain today are these people and their descendants. In recent decades, many Muslims have moved to Britain to escape persecution or violence in countries such as Somalia, Afghanistan, Iraq and Iran. There are also many white Muslims who were originally from Eastern Europe, as well as a small number of people who have converted to Islam from Christianity or no faith. This means that there is no such thing as a 'typical' Muslim, just as there is no such thing as a typical Jew, Christian or atheist.

Different groups of Muslims share many beliefs. However, there are also some differences and disagreements about what it means to be a Muslim in Britain. One of the reasons for this is that each community has brought parts of its own national identity or culture with it. These cultural differences affect the way in which Muslims practise their religion. Muslims from Pakistan or Iraq may have a different understanding of Islam from Muslims from Bosnia or Bangladesh. For example, they may disagree about whether women should cover their heads in public.

Muslims work in a variety of jobs in Britain. Many are successful athletes and some have represented Britain in sports such as cricket and athletics. Others have become successful business leaders, comedians, musicians, doctors, lawyers and politicians.

Modern challenges

Since the terrorist attacks on the USA by Islamic militants in 2001, many Muslims living in mainly Christian or secular societies have experienced rising levels of **Islamophobia**. This situation has worsened in recent years because of other terrorist attacks. Some people argue that poor reporting of Islam in the media has further encouraged negative stereotypes and discrimination. They say that it is unfair to judge the majority of peace-loving Muslims on the violent actions of a small group and that these militants' actions are against the message of Islam.

> **Fact**
>
> Although most Muslims started moving to Britain in the second half of the twentieth century, a few hundred Muslims lived in sixteenth-century Elizabethan England. One of Queen Elizabeth's favourite servants was a young Muslim girl who advised her on shoe fashion.

In 2016, Londoners voted for Sadiq Khan to be the first Muslim mayor of London.

Many people think that negative coverage of Islam in the media is one reason for the rise of Islamophobia.

Islamophobia

The word 'Islamophobia' is a neologism – a new word or expression that has entered the English language. 'Phobia' means either a fear or dislike of something. Islamophobia describes the way in which some people dislike, discriminate and are prejudiced against, Muslims because of their religion.

In recent years, there has been an increase in Islamophobic crime in Britain. This can involve verbal, physical or online abuse of Muslims. However, some people dislike the word 'Islamophobia', and argue that it may prevent people from making fair criticisms of Islam. For example, if someone says that it is wrong for women to be made to wear headscarves in conservative Islamic countries, he or she may be accused of being 'Islamophobic'. However, critics say that in free societies all religions and beliefs should be debated and that criticising a religion is not the same as making generalisations about whole groups of people.

Other challenges

Followers of a minority religion often live in the same area. There are many practical reasons for this. It is convenient for Muslims to live in an area where there is a mosque and other amenities, such as halal butchers and restaurants. However, this can limit the number of areas where Muslims might choose to live.

At some schools in Britain, like this primary school in London, the majority of pupils are Muslims.

In Muslim-majority countries, it is usual for men pray at the mosque at noon on Friday. However, in Britain, this can be difficult if someone has a job that requires him or her to be working at this time. Equally, in many Muslim-majority countries, there are public holidays during the month of Ramadan, but this is not the case in the UK. This means that people have to attend work or school while fasting.

When sending children to school in Britain, Muslim parents might be keen to ensure that they will be able to eat halal food and that the sports kit they wear is modest. They might also be concerned that the pull of secular ideas and lifestyles could cause their children to take Islam less seriously, or even abandon it. In some communities, it could bring shame on a family if a child abandoned the family's faith. This could cause children to feel like they have betrayed their culture or let their parents down.

In a multi-faith society, a Muslim may wish to marry someone of a different religion, against his or her parents' wishes. This could cause conflict in a family and difficulties for the couple when choosing a location to get married. Living different religious lives and deciding in which religion to bring up their own children could also cause problems. For the children, it could be confusing knowing which religion, if any, they should follow.

Key vocabulary

Islamophobia A word meaning 'a fear or dislike of Muslims'; disliking and discriminating against Muslims because of their religion

Check your understanding

1 What percentage of the British population are Muslims?

2 How has Islam become the second-largest religion in the UK?

3 What might Muslims in Britain disagree about and why?

4 What is Islamophobia and why do some people dislike the term?

5 'Islamophobia is the main challenge facing Muslims in Britain today.' Discuss this statement.

Unit 2: Islam in the modern world
Knowledge organiser

Key vocabulary

adhan The call to prayer

Ashura A festival in which Shi'a Muslims mourn the death of Ali's son Hussein at the Battle of Karbala

burkini Swimwear worn by Muslim women to maintain modesty; it was banned in 20 French towns in 2016

burqa A cloak that covers the body from head to toe, often with a mesh screen to see through

Eid ul-Adha A four-day celebration in the final month of the Islamic year

Eid ul-Fitr A three-day celebration after Ramadan

feminist Someone who argues for women's rights and believes women are not being treated equally

Five Pillars Five important acts of worship in a Muslim's life, which form the basis of the faith

Hadith The reported sayings of Muhammad, heard by people during his life and written down in the centuries after his death

hajj A pilgrimage to Mecca

halal Permitted

haram Forbidden

hijab A scarf that covers some or all of the head and hair, but not the face

ihram The state of holiness or purity entered into by pilgrims before beginning hajj

imam A word used by Shi'a Muslims to refer to Ali and his 11 descendants. It also means the leader of prayers in a Sunni mosque

Islamophobia A word meaning 'a fear or dislike of Muslims'; disliking and discriminating against Muslims because of their religion

jihad Literally, 'struggle'; this can be physical or spiritual

mihrab An alcove in a mosque wall showing the direction of Mecca

militants Individuals or groups who use violence to spread their ideas

minaret A mosque tower from which the muezzin traditionally gives the adhan

minbar A platform in a mosque from which the imam delivers his sermon

muezzin A person responsible for performing the adhan in a mosque

niqab A cloth that covers the head and face except the eyes

patriarchal A word used to describe a society where men have more power and control than women

pilgrimage A journey taken to a place of religious importance

prostrating Bowing with part of the body above the knees touching the floor, e.g. hands

salah Prayers that Muslims must perform five times a day

sawm Fasting during the month of Ramadan

secular Non-religious

Shahadah The Muslim declaration of faith – there is no god but God, and Muhammad is his messenger

Shari'a law Guidance on all aspects of life for Muslims, from the three main sources of authority – the Qur'an, Sunnah and Hadith

ummah The global community of Muslims

wudu Ritual washing before prayer

zakah The act of giving 2.5 per cent of your savings to charity

Key facts

- There are five practices, known as the Five Pillars of Islam, that are central to life as a Muslim. The first and most important is the Shahadah (declaration of faith).

- The second pillar is salah (prayer five times a day). In mosques, a muezzin gives the adhan from either inside the mosque or from one of the minarets so that people know it is time to pray. Muslims perform wudu (washing) before praying and pray facing the direction of Mecca.

- During the month of Ramadan, Muslims fast from sunrise to sunset. The 30 days of fasting are followed by a celebration called Eid ul-Fitr. Those who are ill, elderly, young, pregnant or travelling do not have to fast.

- Hajj is a pilgrimage to Mecca that every Muslim tries to undertake during the course of his or her lifetime. Before arriving in Mecca, pilgrims enter the state of ihram and wear white cotton clothes. In order to become a hajji or hajja, pilgrims must circle the Ka'aba, walk or run between the hills of Marwah and Safa, pray for forgiveness on Mount Arafat and stone Satan at Mina. Approximately three million Muslims go on hajj each year. The pilgrimage lasts for five days in the last month of the Islamic year.

- Despite many similarities, Sunni and Shi'a Muslims have different beliefs and practices. Over the course of history, there have been violent clashes between Sunni and Shi'a Muslims, and these continue today.

- Shari'a law (based on the Qur'an, Hadith and Sunnah) teaches Muslims what is halal (permitted). Anything that is not halal is haram (forbidden).

- The question of whether Muslim women should wear a hijab, niqab, burqa or burkini causes much controversy, both within and outside Islam.

- The majority of Muslims view jihad (which means struggle) as a personal struggle to live a good life as a Muslim (the 'greater jihad'). They condemn the views and actions of Islamic militants.

- Five per cent of people in Britain follow Islam. There were some Muslims in Elizabethan England, but most moved to Britain in the second half of the twentieth century. Muslims in Britain today face a number of challenges, including Islamophobia.

Muslims celebrating Eid ul-Fitr.

Index

Acknowledgements

Every effort has been made to trace copyright holders and to obtain their permission for the use of copyright material.

The publishers will gladly receive any information enabling them to rectify any error or omission at the first opportunity.

The publishers would like to thank the following for permission to reproduce copyright material:

(t = top, b = bottom, c = centre, l = left, r = right)

Text

QUR'AN BILINGUAL, REVISED EDITION translated by M.A.S. Abdel Haleem (2010). Used with permission of Oxford University Press.

Photographs

Cover and title page Zoran Karapancev/Shutterstock, pp6–7 Maciej Dakowicz/Alamy Stock Photo, p8 Jlimages/Alamy Stock Photo, p11 Zuma Press, Inc./Alamy Stock Photo, p12 t Anadolu Agency/Getty images, p12 b arabianEye FZ LLC/Alamy Stock Photo, p13 Atif Saeed/Alamy Stock Photo, p14 Art Directors & TRIP/Alamy Stock Photo, p15 Caroline Penn/Alamy Stock Photo, p16 Dan Kitwood/Getty Images, p17 Picture Partners/Alamy Stock Photo, p18 t Eddie Gerald/Alamy Stock Photo, p18 b Photo Researchers, Inc/Alamy Stock Photo, p19 Godong/Universal Images Group via Getty Images, p20 Classic Image/Alamy Stock Photo, p21 B.O'Kane/Alamy Stock Photo, p22 UniversalImagesGroup/Getty Images, p23 Shahhh/Wikimedia Commons, p24 jlimages/Alamy Stock Photo, pp26–27 Anadolu Agency/Getty images, p28 Godong/Alamy Stock Photo, p29 Mehmet Biber/DPA/PA Images, p30 Eric Lafforgue/Art in All of Us/Getty Images, p31 t ZouZou/Shutterstock, p31 b Lukas Hlavac/Shutterstock, p32 irinaorel/Shutterstock, p33 t Nana Safiana/Newzulu/Alamy Live News, p33 b arabianEye FZ LLC/Alamy Stock Photo, p34 t REUTERS/Alamy Stock Photo, p34 BL gulf eye/Shutterstock, p36 Mohammed Sawaf/AFP/Getty Images, p37 t Haidar Mohammed Ali/AFP/Getty Images, p37 b Lenscap Photography/Shutterstock.com, p38 t Taraskin/Shutterstock, p38 c Clari Massimiliano/Shutterstock, p38 b Thomas Imo/Alamy Stock Photo, p39 l dpa picture alliance archive/Alamy Stock Photo, p39 r Kzenon/Alamy Stock Photo, p41 Sean Dempsey PA Archive/PA Images, p42 t Rupert Rivett/Alamy Stock Photo, p42 b Mike Kemp/Getty Images, p43 Gideon Mendel/Getty Images, p45 Nisarg Lakhmani/Alamy Stock Photo.